Two T

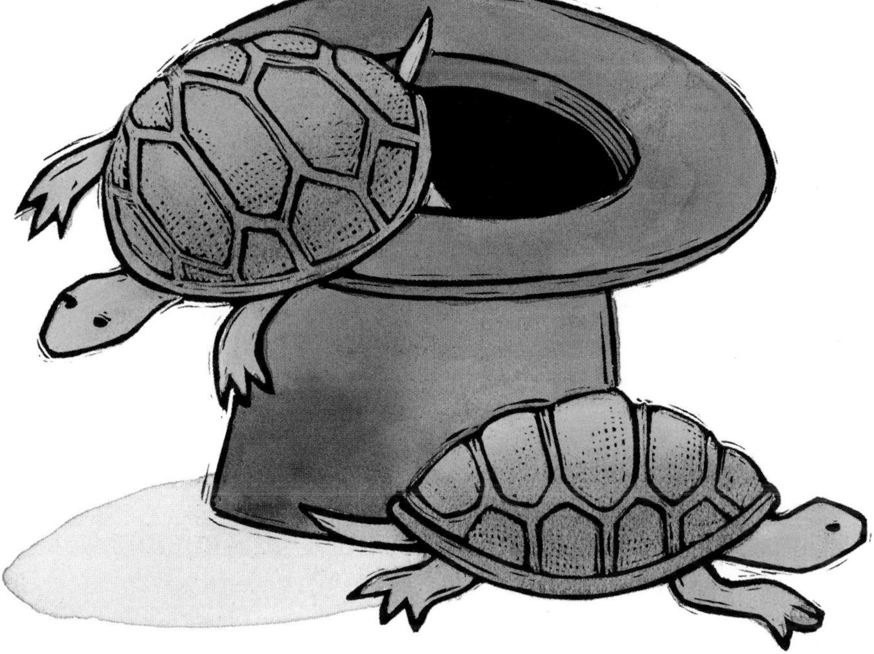

Written by Carly Easton
Illustrated by Katherine Tillotson

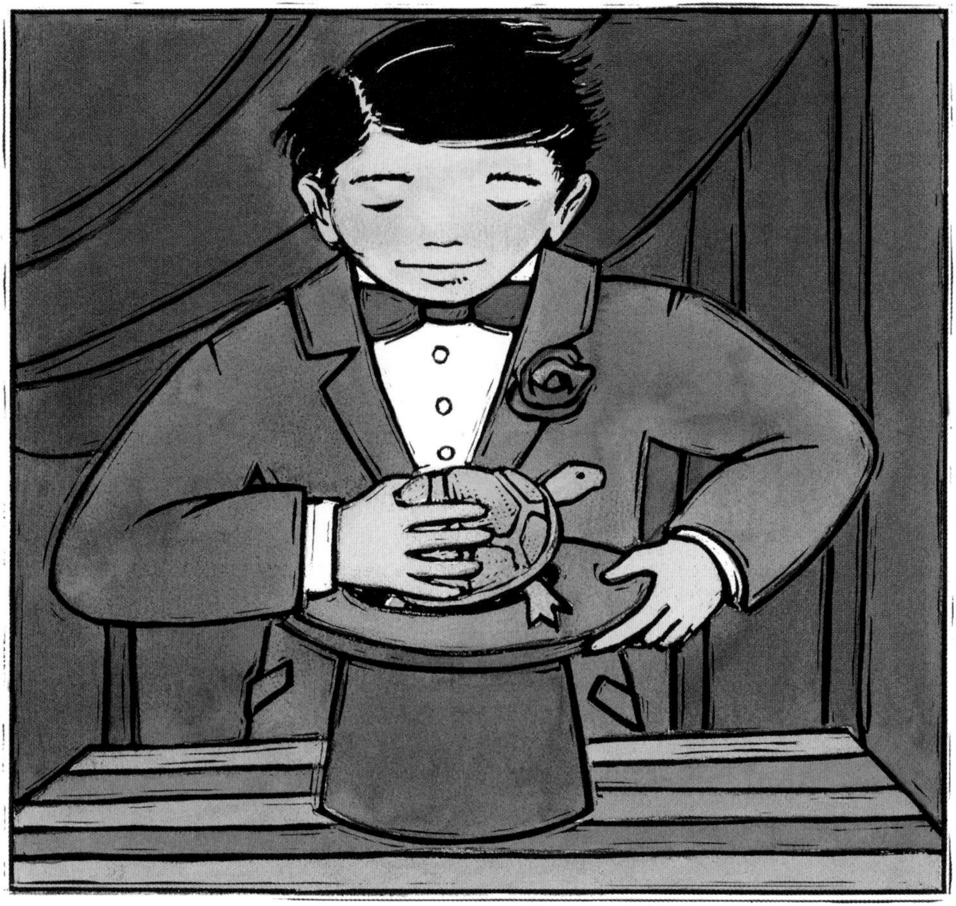

One turtle,

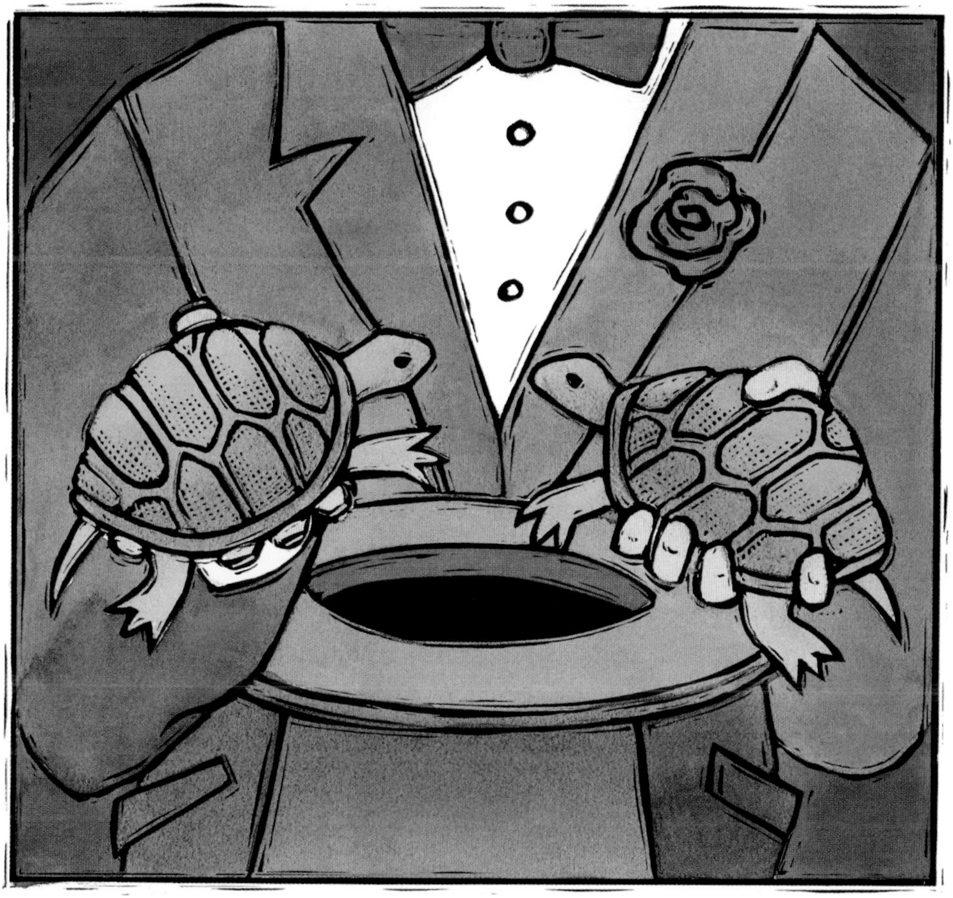

two turtles.

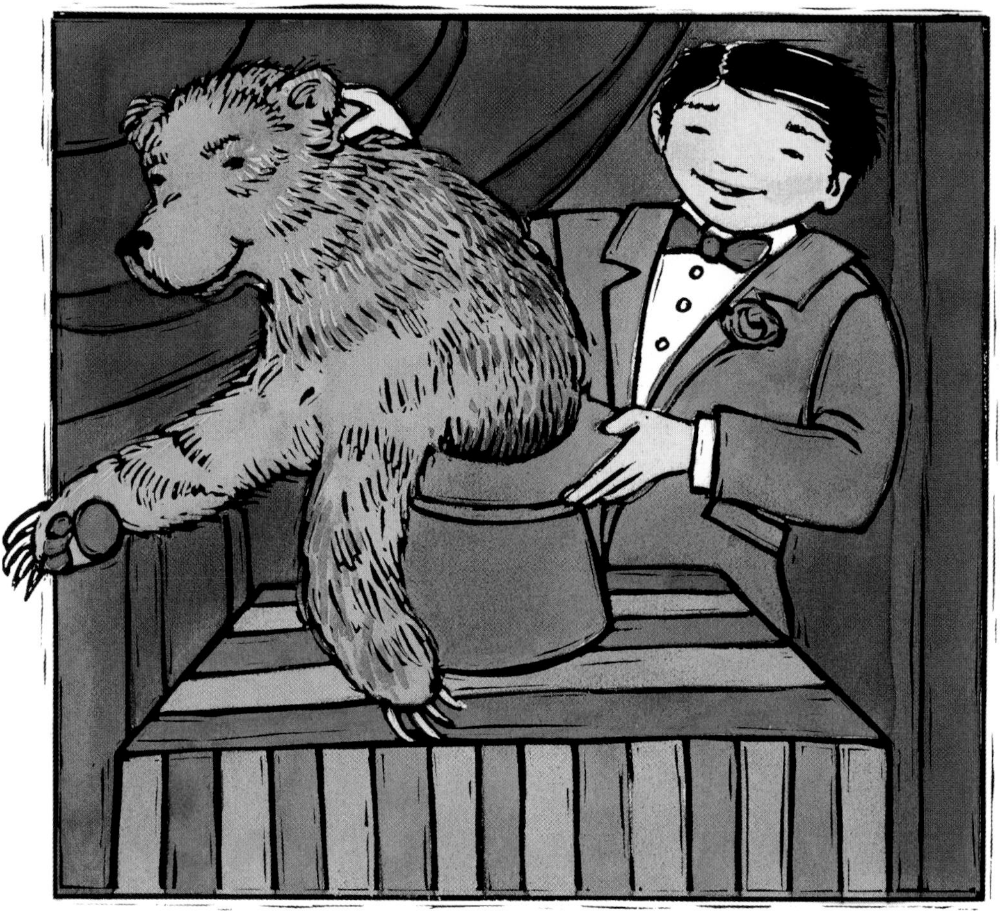

One bear,

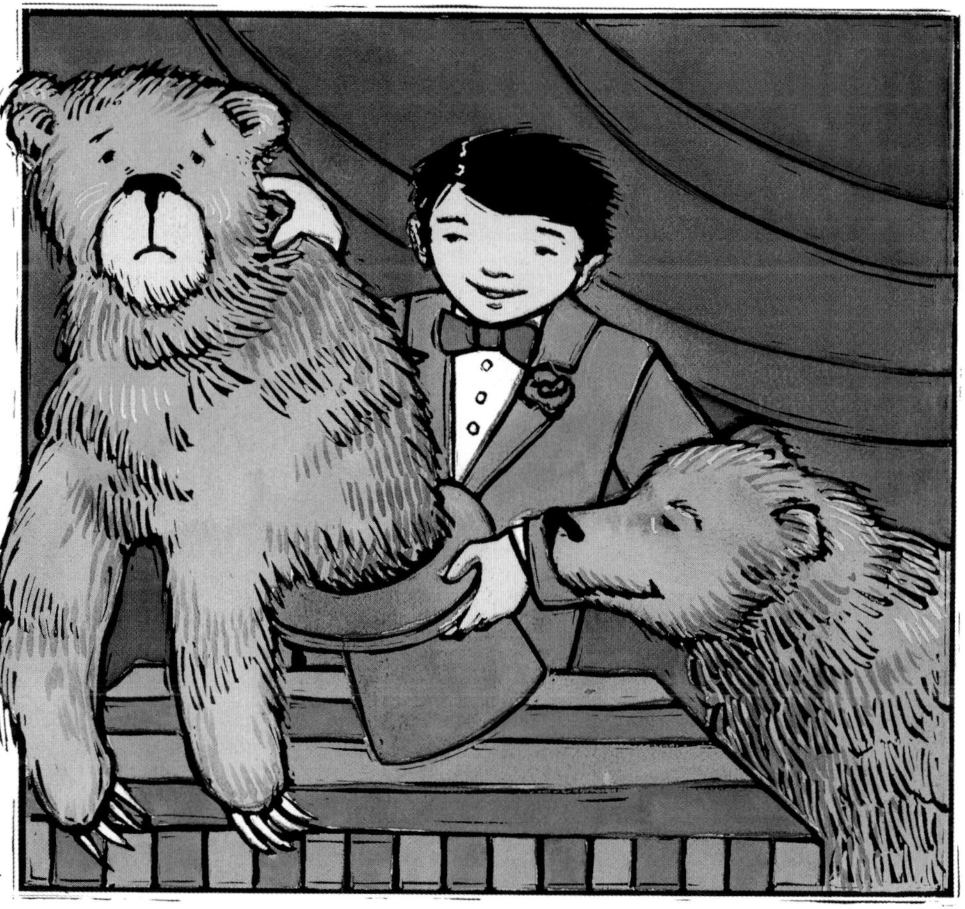

two bears.

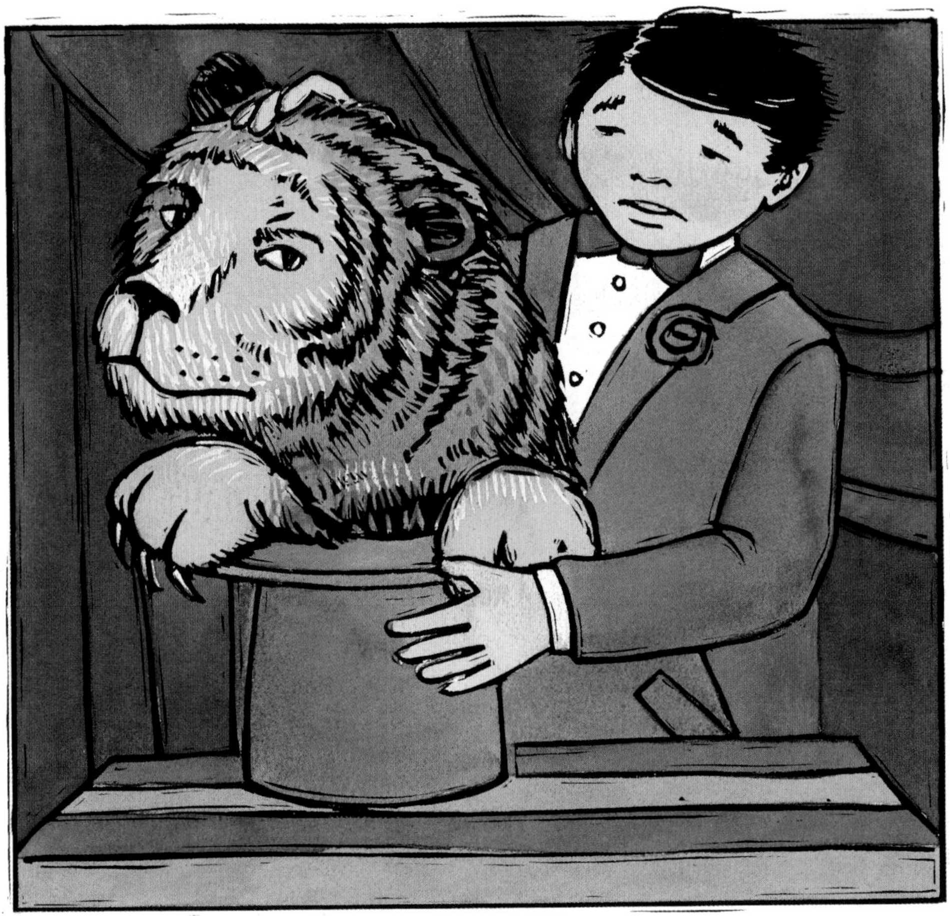

One tiger,

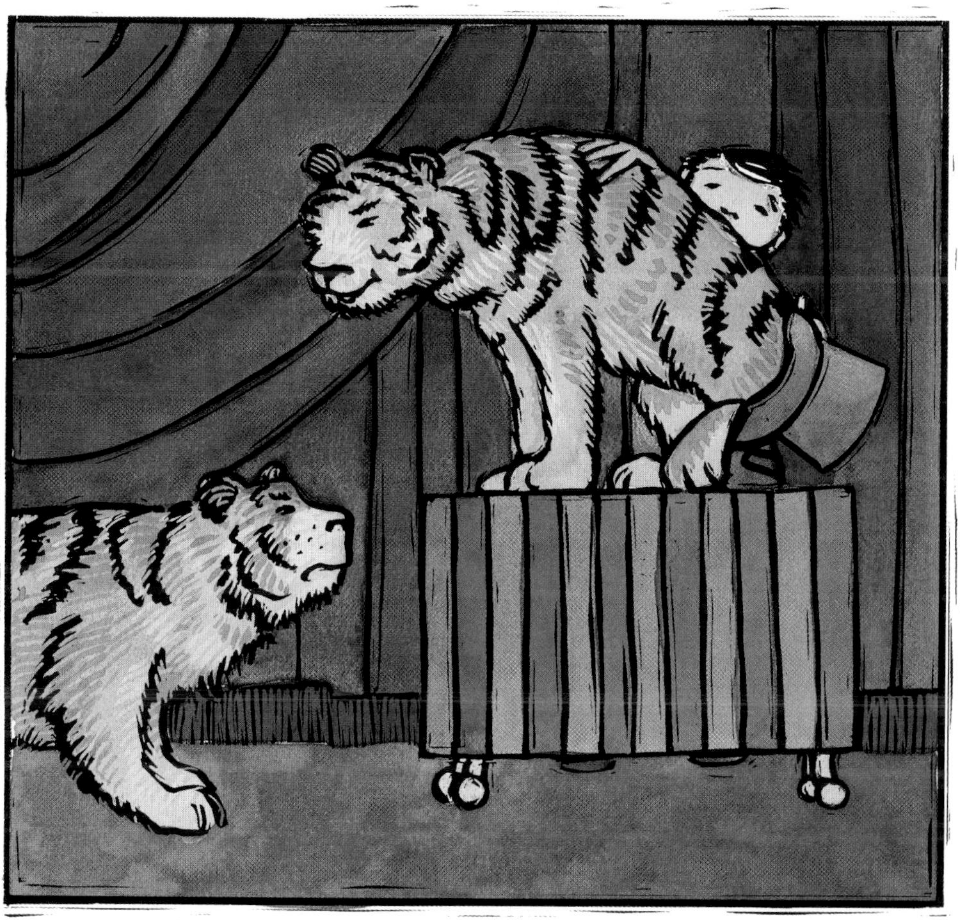

two tigers.

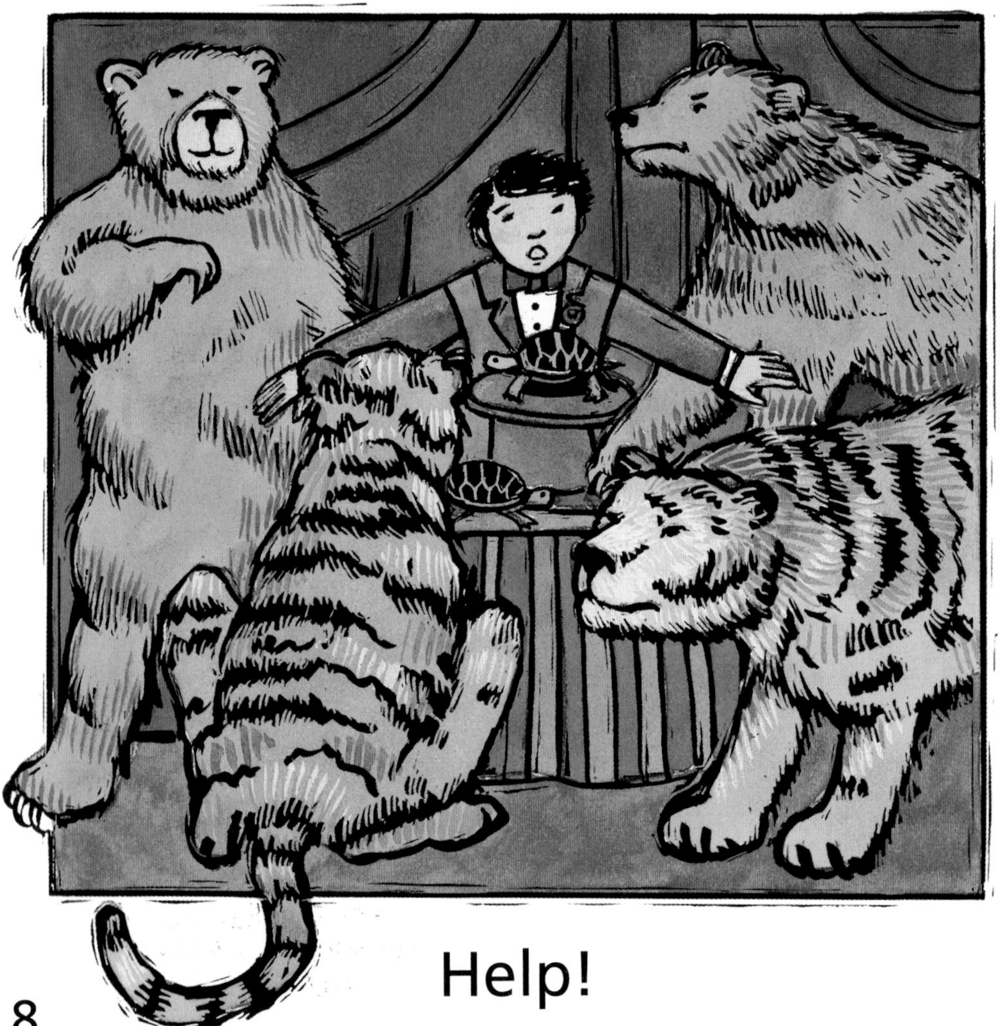

Help!